Elemental

Earth - Water - Air - Fire

Contents

For the good people of St Luke's in Holloway, north London...

from whom we steal our stuff.

Elemental

Earth - Water - Air - Fire

Stuff. Matter. The stuff that matters. The stuff that has always mattered.

So elemental are earth, water, air and fire that most of the time we don't give them a second thought. They're so visible they've become invisible.

Until they go missing. At which point they reappear in our consciousness: as soon as we can't walk on it, drink it, breathe it or feel its heat, we notice how inextricably our presence is tied up with each of these primal partners.

But while every element has an irreplaceable, functional role in our existence, each also carries multiple layers of other meanings. So, when we were asked to give a series of talks in Holloway, north London we decided to dig into, drink in, inhale and fire ourselves with this rich material.

The result is this slight book, in which the four classical elements turn out to be about more than physical survival. They raise questions about who we are, what we're made of... and why we're here.

Stuff. Matter. The stuff that matters.

The stuff of life.

Earth - Water - Air - Fire

Malcolm Doney and Martin Wroe
November 2009

"Life on earth, the life of the spirit. Food and drink, heart and soul, it's all part of the same thing. We are material girls and boys, called to get our hands dirty."

Earth

My bladder is roughly half-pint size, like
the rest of me. So, when I'm sleeping in a
tent – like I was at the Greenbelt arts festival recently – and I've been to the beer tent
earlier in the evening, there comes a time
in the middle of the night when a wrestling
match takes place.

The contest is between the beer, bladder
capacity, the cold earth, the warm bed, the
sharp night air, muscular control, mental

exertion and the idea of stumbling out into a floodlit field where strange people are still wandering at large. And where the long shadow of a short man peeing is cast like a huge screen image on someone else's tent. In the end, with me, the bladder always wins. You can't ignore your body.

Here I was, at a festival which celebrates the spirit; in which people were gathered to explore ways in which we encounter God. We were considering all sorts of huge ideas – yet again and again, I was aware that my feet were sore, or that the grass was damp, or that sitting cross-legged is really uncomfortable, or that I needed a steak and ale pie.

We're physical people, with physical needs in a physical universe. Which is why I want to think about earth. And I love it.

 I love the very word earth, it's rich, crumbly, fertile, organic, alive. It's solid, dependable, firm, foundational, nutritional. You can grow in earth, build

with it, shape it and fire it, tunnel through it, hollow it out. And I love all the synonyms for earth: dirt, sod, soil, mud, ground, terrain, terra, gaia, tilth, humus. The earth is our home, we are earthy, grounded, rooted people.

As it says in the book of Genesis, we are taken from the ground: "you are dust and to dust you shall return."

This is a good thing, especially for someone like me who finds prayer and silent meditation almost impossible. Trying to absorb myself into the mind of God like the mystics do, does my head in… I am in awe of people who can go into that zone.

I'm not suggesting for a moment that people who are gifted or disciplined enough to encounter God in a rich inner life are somehow otherworldly. At best, such people are rounded, whole individuals who achieve a balance between all the parts of themselves. But what I do want to do is to affirm the fact that earthiness is OK. That earth and body, and soul and spirit, and heart and mind, are all healthily mixed up. God can speak to us from the bottom up.

The body is not simply a temporary shell for the soul to live in, as if the soul was the real thing and the body simply packaging. This idea still has currency among many 'religious' or 'spiritual' people, but it breeds an unhealthy separation, and hierarchy, between spirit and flesh. Psychologist Guy Claxton, in his marvellous book, *The Wayward Mind* talks about the way we are inclined to think of our souls as a "buried scrap of divinity, the immaculate memento of [God's] glory, which [he has] hidden in every human heart".

But Caxton argues that you can't divorce the soul or spirit from the rest of who we are. It's actually intertwined with the rest of

us. It's to do with being joined up with the air we breathe, the food we eat, the culture that nurtures us, the families who raise us, as well as the God who dwells within us. It's part he says of the "relationship with *this* world of wood and gristle and fellow feeling". Good word, gristle – it's tactile and chewy and this-worldly.

The me-ness of me, the you-ness of you. The mind, the heart, the self, the personality, is not located in one place. It is embodied, embedded, incarnated. The fact that we are earthed is the reason that place, genes, family, ethnicity, nation, culture and friendship are elemental to us. For instance, just think, how would you spend your Sunday morning if you had been brought up in India or Japan, or Thailand, or Tehran, or Haifa? The Spirit, like a river, follows channels that are already there.

We are a complex – a bundle of instincts, animal urges, emotions and gut belief which can defy reason. The whole of our being is respond- ing to a mass of stimuli – and these include the cycles and rhythms of nature.

I know I'm an ignorant townie, but it always amazes me that plants know what season it is and what to do to respond to it. My horse Neville is growing a winter coat, the leaves are falling from the trees. The ground is getting itself ready for the repeating cycle of life, death and rebirth. My body, my soul, knows it too.

As the poet RS Thomas writes in *Suddenly*:

"…the weather
is [God's] mind's turbine
driving the earth's bulk round
and around on its remedial journey."

This echoes the thoughts of an earlier, more famous poet, William Wordsworth. In his *Lines written a few miles above Tintern Abbey*, he detects in the earth:

"A presence that disturbs me with the joy
Of elevated thoughts; a sense sublime
Of something far more deeply
interfused…
…A motion and a spirit, that impels
All thinking things, all objects of all
thought,
And rolls through all things."

Mind, spirit, unconscious, self. Is this just so much brain activity? No, says Caxton, it is "intrinsically more mysterious, more embodied". What Guy Caxton is saying chimes with an idea of who we are that we find buried and often un-noticed and unseen in the earth of the Old Testament. There's a Hebrew word which I have become really excited by since I discovered it. It is *Nephesh*. It's one of those words which is pretty much untranslateable as a single word directly into English.

It appears in the Old Testament some 754 times, and in many older Bible translations it's mostly translated as "soul". It is also translated as any one of 44

different words or phrases. Now, to say that it – *Nephesh* – is soul (particularly given our rather spiritualised take on it) is both inexact and misleading. The Hebrew idea of soul is much more embodied and much more to do with our human identity. *Nephesh* can be rendered as *life, heart, being, person, the centre of vitality, the lust for life* and, since it is also translated as '*throat*' it can be seen as the *thirst for God*. It's a rich deep, loamy word – like earth.

When we read in Genesis that God formed man from the dust of the ground and breathed into his nostrils the breath of life, the man became a living soul, or being, that word is *Nephesh*.

Nephesh is at the seat of who we are and our deepest longings, and desires and appetites and actions. Psychologist Tory Hoff says, "In Hebrew the soul is the man. Indeed we should not say that man has a soul, but that he is a soul; nor consequently that he has a body, but that he is a body." We are people of the earth.

That's why a dodgy curry affects your prayer life. Or why on a soggy evening in February, God seems to be entirely absent. It's why we are are smitten by strange sensations. The poet AE Houseman once said, "Experience has shown me, when I am shaving in the morning, to keep watch over my thoughts, because if a line of poetry strays into my memory, my skin bristles so that the razor ceases to act."

One of my favourite of Jesus' miracles is the one recounted in the Gospel of John where he literally gets his hands dirty. Jesus, who the church tends to make all wafty and lah-di-dah, leans over and gobs on the ground. He bends down, and mixes up a mud-pack of earth and spittle, and slaps it on the eyes of the blind man who has asked for healing. Extraordinary. It's earth and spirit, body and soul all in one *Nephesh-y* job lot. That's healing and wholeness for you.

In fact if you look at Jesus' life and work you see that this earthy, interconnection of flesh and spirit is at the heart of who he is. When he talks about bringing good news to "the poor", for instance these are not simply people without money (though they are included). The reason they are poor might be economic, spiritual, physical, religious, social or political or a combination of any of these. Their poverty is demonstrated in their exclusion, their rejection, their lost-ness. And salvation is a reversal of their circumstances, much more than a simple faith formula. It is rich and nuanced and earthed.

RS Thomas is one of the world's gloomiest Welshmen, and that's saying something. But in that poem, *Suddenly*, quoted above, his soul stirs into lyricism at the earth. This is a man whose poems are a darkly glorious record of arriving at places where God has just left. Yet here, he finds that:

"He addresses me from a myriad
directions with the fluency
of water, the articulateness
of green leaves; and in the genes,
too, the components of my existence.
The rock, so long speechless, is the library
of his poetry."

In church, people eat bread and drink
wine, to remember Jesus who came from
Nazareth, a plot of ground, a place on a
map. He was someone who handled wood
for a living. Who wrote messages with his
finger in the dust, who spat on the ground.
Who took his friends' feet, caked and
crusted with dirt, and washed them with
water and dried them with a towel. Who
was beaten up and stripped. Who was
stretched across planks, and hung up to
die. As a result we meet God. On Earth.

Life on earth, the life of the spirit. Food
and drink, heart and soul, it's all
part of the same thing. We are
material girls and boys, called,
like Jesus, to get our hands dirty.

With RS Thomas we can find ourselves listening to the things around us – weeds, stones, the earth itself, "speaking to us in the vernacular of the purposes of One who is".

The Australian poet Les Murray puts it another way. He says that through our experiences, we receive "ordinary mail of the otherworld, wholly common, not post-marked divine". This idea of the divine speaking to us through stuff, though the earth, in the vernacular makes so much sense to me. It affirms who we are, where we come from, what we do, what we feel, what our bodies are telling us.

So when your bladder calls you in the middle of the night. It's the earthiness speaking. And it might be worth listening.

"Like God herself, water was never far from your thoughts … but not always particularly accessible."

Water

From London N7, it would take about 60 minutes on foot. On a bus you could be there in 20. If you live in this city, it's one way to tell if you are north or south. Without it, we wouldn't be here... but we only share it. Along with millions of others.

The River Thames is London's river. But it's more than that. At 215 miles long, it stretches from its source near Cirencester all the way across England via Oxford and

Reading and Maidenhead, via scores of other villages and towns, before arriving on the edge of the capital. From Teddington to Richmond to Kew it snakes down to the Palace of Westminster and then moves effortlessly on to Greenwich and the Isle of Dogs, out to Dartford and Gravesend until finally morphing into an estuary and heading into the North Sea near Southend.

Unless you're at its edge, most of the time you can't see the Thames from many of the villages and towns it cuts through. You can't see it from most of London. Yet without it, London and all those places, wouldn't be here.

Some things are essential for life even though most of the time we remain blithely unaware of them. Air, fire, earth… and water. The four elements.

 London is here because one day, several thousand years ago, some ancient Ray Mears type realised that the banks of this

river provided an ideal place to set up camp: water to drink and grow crops with, fish to eat, a ready-made route to paddle along. Access to water has been the key to survival throughout history. Great cities were founded by the waters edge, from Cairo on the Nile to Jericho on the Jordan, from Paris on the Seine to New York on the Hudson. "London" itself may be derived from a celtic word 'Lyndon', which means "shadowy waters". The Thames.

Living in the city, we don't think of ourselves as river folk or water people-even though some primeval instinct for ocean views and sea-air sends us off to the coast for holidays. The best way to get close to the water in my patch of London is to walk down Caledonian Road or Camden Road until you reach a bridge crossing Regents Canal, then slip off the road and wind along the water for miles. Follow the water to Paddington and you could join the Grand Union Canal. Give yourself a few days and you could walk along the waters edge for 137 miles, all the way to Birmingham.

That's a secret journey now, but in earlier times and in ancient literature much more of life was on the water. You can trace this in the aphorisms we use, subliminally handed down in our cultural traditions. Language often uncovers our hidden history. Few of us go fishing for example but we talk easily of someone being "a fish out of water". Rarely do our lakes and rivers freeze over but still we talk of people "skating on thin ice". Exasperated with someone we've tried to support but who evidently imagines they can manage alone, we don't say "I've done all I can, it's obvious what he needs to do, its up to him…" Instead we mysteriously dredge up some ancient equine cliché: "You can lead a horse to water but you can't make him drink." As if we were stable owners or horse whisperers.

Water has soaked our language and culture

 from the beginning. In its opening poem, in a time before time had been thought of, the Bible describes a river flowing from the Garden of Eden. And with

the final poem of the book, the Book of Revelation, set in a time after time is no longer thought of, we come back to a river – the river of the water of life flowing from a divine throne. It's the same as the one in Eden, providing sustenance for a tree of life which bears good fruit – a tree of life whose leaves, as Revelation puts it, "are for the healing of the nations".

In the alternative history of faith, in which we find ourselves, life begins with water and ends with water. And while the waters of the Bible are sometimes a warning, such as in the Flood, more often than not water punctuates this sacred history as a blessing, a cleansing, a healing balm and a baptism which promises a new start.

Strange then, that with such a noble history, we no longer give water a second thought. Maybe it's because it's now on tap. We notice our need for it only when we are parched and then, most of the time, it's within easy reach. Few of us have been scarily thirsty – where we couldn't see where the next drink was coming from. Where water had once again, momentarily reminded itself of its true worth, literally more valuable than gold.

The Bible emerged in a culture unlike ours, a hot middle eastern world where getting water was the most vital task of the day. Water was not on tap and people were thirsty a lot of the time. Water was deep down a well and needed to be drawn up in a bucket, slowly and surely. Or it was a hot, dusty walk away at the river. Like God herself, water was never far from your thoughts … but not always particularly accessible.

The thought gave rise to a great simile, the idea of thirst as longing.
"As the hart panteth after the water brooks", says the Psalmist, "so panteth my soul after thee, O God".

A double simile actually: the thirst for God like the thirst for water, and the picture of the deer, tongue hanging out,

slurping with relief at the edge of the brook.

Jesus is parched and panting like a deer on a day that he famously sits down by a well. He's been out in the country, spinning stories, answering questions, wondering what his calling is and, as he hasn't yet got a decent answer, he's heading back to Galilee. Tired, hot. Parched.

The midday sun is burning and he sits down by this well.

As it turns out, because this is a story from the Bible, it's not just any well. It's Jacob's Well, a legendary source of water, springing deep underground, to which generations of people had come to wind up the cool, clean liquid from the dark depths below. You can still find it today, in the town of Nablus, in Palestine.

Usually, it was women who came for the water, like the sassy Samaritan in the story that John tells, a foreign woman in

Israel carrying her bucket to take water back to her family, just as Agnes is carrying her water in Malawi right now, and Grace in Mozambique and Blessings in Uganda. Just like women and girls all over the world have watered humanity down the millennia. Just as right now they are balancing water like life on their shoulder or back or head, walking through fields, along dusty roads, taking life in a bucket or carton back to the village, to cook the evening meal or to drink tomorrow morning.

Jesus knows this woman is thirsty. And she knows Jesus is thirsty. She is witty and bold, and holds an advantage. She has a bucket and he doesn't.

Maybe she gets him a drink… but Jesus has something to offer too. As she reels up the water which will keep her children alive, he offers to sate another kind of

 thirst – one just as deep and desperate as that for water. I can offer you living water, he says, you'll never be thirsty again. It will be like your own internal

spring he says, a source of divine sustenance bursting with eternal life.

Everyone of us is thirsty.

Is there a connection between the two
kinds of thirst, for physical and for spiritual
sustenance? Is there a connection between
the water we drink and the water that our
sisters and brothers in so many countries
today cannot drink? Because it is scarce or
contaminated or, thanks to climate-change
related drought, increasingly absent.

A clue is found in the story of Henry
Whitehead. In 1854, in the West End of
London, there was an outbreak of disease.
Looking back, it was inevitable: people
lived in overcrowded, squalid conditions
with cesspools overrunning into the streets
and a great torrent of human waste
permanently diverted into the River
Thames, which had become an
open sewer.

London stank. Really stank. In
August of 1854, 127 people

near Broad Street – now called Broadwick – died in three days. Within a week 500 had died. People were terrified and began to flee, cholera stalked every home. It wasn't surprising that London was so smelly, what with all the human waste. You find the same in shanty towns in developing countries today. It's hard not to hold your nose as you walk through. We're not used to it.

In the 19th century, people connected the bad smell with the outbreaks of killer disease – they thought cholera was a miasma, that it spread through bad air, that if you breathed it you caught it. That was the medical orthodoxy. But there was a dissenting voice, a man called John Snow, who suspected foul air was not the culprit – he thought it might be to do with the water supply. Bad water, not bad air. It's a story brilliantly told in Steven Johnson's book

The Ghost Map: the story of London's most terrifying epidemic an how it changed science, cities and the modern world. Although everybody thought he was nuts, Snow

had a hunch that the source of this cholera outbreak was a single public water pump on Broadwick Street.

Unfortunately he couldn't prove anything… until he met someone who knew most people in the area, knew which houses had seen deaths and which had not – and also knew which routes people took to which water pumps. More important still, he was happy to walk around the streets of Soho asking questions and getting answers, helping Snow map the outbreak of the disease. Noting which households had lost members, which had not, which used certain water pumps, which did not.

This man was the Revd Henry Whitehead, local vicar of St Luke's church in Soho and, over time, he worked with the scientist Snow to provide statistical evidence that the Broadwick Street pump was the source of the outbreak. In short – although it took years – between them they changed the prevailing medical orthodoxy, showing that cholera spreads not through air but through water. Water which has been contaminated by human waste.

To cut a long and quietly heroic story even shorter, the work of the two men accelerated both the birth of the science of epidemiology and the birth of modern sewage systems. In time, waste was no longer diverted into rivers like the Thames, spreading disease across the country, but kept separate from the water supply and treated in sewage plants.

Henry Whitehead believed that the route to satisfying our own spiritual thirst lay in relieving the thirst of others, that being part of the Church was inevitably about healing the wounds of our shared world.

Thirst.

 Perhaps it's why some of us become part of the Church. It doesn't add any obvious value to our CVs, doesn't get us points on a course, or kudos with the

neighbours. It's neither particularly exhilarating or trailblazing.

Maybe it's about thirst. For friendship, for community, for clues about life's journey… for things we might not even have words for. Communities of faith can be like wells, where we hope to draw sustenance from the dim source of Christian tradition, or the mysterious depths of each others lives.

You cannot bottle it. It is not on tap. You have to go back to the well, again and again and again. Sometimes the bucket will come up empty. Sometimes a bit murky and dubious. You might need to boil it first.

Sometimes, though, you will bring up the water of life: as you talk with your neighbours; as you put yourself in their story; as you sit and pray; as you sing songs or listen to readings; as you contemplate the faces of those around you, young and old, lonesome or welcomed, curious or confused. Sometimes you will

taste the living water Jesus talked about;
you will sense a well bursting in your heart;
you will feel replenished and ready for the
rest of the journey.

Sometimes.

The local churches or communities of faith
which we share are each of them small
encampments by a well, little villages
nestling on a tributary of the great river of
faith that runs from the past and meanders
into the future. A river that runs from a
far-distant source in the Garden of Eden,
via ancient cultures and strange geogra-
phies, via matriarchs and patriarchs, priests
and prophets, teachers and healers all the
while winding its strange course through
saints and sinners we have never heard of
and lapping near the feet of our own
parents and of us and running quietly but
surely by for our children and their

children and running on and
into the future and all the way
back to Eden.

And as it rolls surely by through the minutes and the centuries, it is providing quiet sustenance for the tree of life whose leaves are for the healing of the nations. Leaves which deliver clean water to those whose water is dirty; leaves which end disease, which fight climate change and poverty; leaves which listen to those with no voice, which shelter those on the margins and in distress.

When we come down to this river to pray, we do not come for self-help. We come to see if we can be of help to others which is the place where we will find our own healing. In seeking out and serving the needs of others, we will find spiritual sustenance ourselves – we will drink from the water of life. This is what Isaiah, a prophet standing by this great river of faith, three thousand years ago, realised. He put it like this...

"If you...
spend yourselves in behalf of the hungry
and satisfy the needs of the oppressed,
then your light will rise in the darkness,
and your night will become like the
noonday.
The Lord will guide you always;
he will satisfy your needs in a
sun-scorched land
and will strengthen your frame.
You will be like a well-watered garden,
like a spring whose waters never fail..."

"The inspiring breath of God is absorbed into our very being, making us natural makers, able to hope, alive and alert every minute to the myriad possibilities that surround us."

Air

When I told our son Lewis that I was going to be writing something about air, he looked superior and said, "Don't tell me. You're going to say, 'the thing about air is that it's invisible, but even though you can't see it, it's still there and we can't live without it, and that's a bit like God.'"

So that was my first idea out of the window. Kids! You put all that effort into raising them and getting them an

 education and are they grateful? No. They just take the piss out of you.

So, what else can you say about air? Well, the first and most obvious thing is that air is our medium, like water is for fish. And it is true that – even though we can't live without it – we take it pretty much for granted unless, for some reason, we can't breathe. If we find ourselves submerged in water, or choking, having an asthma attack…

We notice air when it's moving of course, when we feel the breeze, or when a strong gust of wind bowls dustbins down the street. And air carries things with it, the waft of perfume from someone's throat, the tang of brine from the ocean, the haze of woodsmoke from a whitewashed cottage.

But now and again we can actually see the air. Some years back, a friend of ours was visiting from Perth in Australia, and he brought his son, Harry, with him, who

must have been about eight. It
was a November morning. They
came straight from the airport
and, shortly after their arrival,
Harry disappeared. I found him
in the garden, sprawled in the hammock,
with a twig in one hand, pretending to
smoke. He lay there absolutely absorbed,
watching the 'smoke' his breath was making in the cold air. I suddenly realised that,
growing up in Western Australia he might
never, ever, have seen his breath before. It
was a moment of total wonder.

Breath of course, is what air is all about.
It's what keeps us alive. Essentially, we
breathe air in, exchange the oxygen for
carbon dioxide and breathe out. It's part of
an unconscious, life-giving rhythm. The
marvel for Harry, that first morning in a
strange land, was that he noticed that he
was breathing, because he could observe it.

The early chapters of the book of Genesis
talk about air in a slightly more mystical
way. Right at the beginning of Genesis, at
the dawn of creation, we read that a wind

 from God swept over the face of the deep – the same word for wind is used for breath – and God *breathed* the world into being, *spoke* it into existence, gave it shape. "God created humankind in his own image… male and female he created them." And as it puts it in chapter two, God breathed life into the nostrils of humankind.

Two fundamentals here. This is theology 1.01. God is a maker, and we are made to reflect the nature of God.

God's response to nothing was to make something. God imagined a universe into being. This idea that we have an imaginative God is of critical importance – not only to our understanding of God, but to our understanding of who we are.

When we read that God "breathed into [man's] nostrils the breath of life", it's an echo of God breathing the world into being. And what – in this poetic account of our origins – does the first human do? He breathes in. This is a big metaphor and rich in meaning. As the eminent critic George Steiner says: "everything having being derives its birth from the intake (the 'inspiration') of God's shaping breath". Human beings are *inspired*. It's an awe-inspiring thought.

So, if we as human beings have breathed in the breath of God, what happens when we breathe out? We breathe out God, in the form of our creativity and imagination. Our response, like God's, is to become makers.

Pre-eminently, that's what we as human beings are: Makers. This is not just about the process of physical invention, like tools, weapons or the wheel. From the very earliest days, we have also generated ideas from the air: routines, plans, cultures.

At the heart of this inspiration to make things is imagination. Imagination is a whole lot more than having the talent to make up stuff. I would argue that it is

perhaps the key element of what it means to be made in the image of God. It is the very air we breathe. We use our imaginations every day, in every sphere of life, and in almost everything we do.

In order for you and me to understand one another, I need to imagine something of what it's like to be you, and vice versa. If I trample over your feelings, it's quite likely that I haven't imagined what it is you're going through. When I cry watching movies, which I do all the time, that's about imagination. Part of the damage of psychosis is that a serial killer can do his work because he cannot imagine the consequences of what he is doing to someone else. He cannot put himself in their place. It's a failure of imagination.

It takes imagination to do any of our making: to develop a road system, to make a garden, to choose a school for our kids, to guess how much garlic to add to the casserole. Almost any decision we make

uses our imagination, which is
rooted in the intake of God's
inspiration, and our attendant
ability to make.

Our faith is built around the imagination
too. Thinking there might be a God in the
first place, and then trying to work out
what God is like. That's why we use
metaphors and similes for God. Is God like
a parent, a monarch, a shepherd… earth,
water, air, fire? Our understanding of who
Jesus was, and what it means to take him as
a model, is rooted in our imagination of
what we think he might be like. To have
any kind of faith at all demands an act of
imagination.

Also, crucially, our ability to hope is
embedded in the imagination. Imagination
– ranging from God's creation, to our own
deeply rooted divine instincts – is to be
alive to possibilities. To ask the important
question which defines who we are: "What
would happen if…"

To hope is to be able to see that things can

 be different, better than they are at the moment. For instance, Nelson Mandela and Desmond Tutu had to imagine another South Africa. Out of that hope came the possibility of re-making the country. We look at Israel/Palestine and hope that something can be made there too. I live in Whitechapel in the East End, and the other day, there were a whole bunch of people gathered into what passes for a park , speechifying, about making life better in Tower Hamlets. These people are alive to new possibilities, they can hope for a better future, because they have imagination.

To ask, "what would happen if…" is as natural as breathing in and out. I'm talking about very everyday stuff – ordinary creativity. It is not just about art. It is just as creative to conjure a meal out of a random selection in your cupboard, or to negotiate with your teenager who's suddenly decided they hate you, or to plunder the mysteries of a misbehaving laptop.

A slight aside here, but being imaginative, being open to new possibilities, isn't about striving after *originality*. The quest for originality is actually a curse.
People who are desperate to be original end up relying on novelty and gimmicks. Genuine originality is about being authentic. It's about trusting in our own uniqueness, the personality God gives us, enmeshed in the tangled web of genes, ethnicity, family background, life experiences, relationship and our own, very particular response to and understanding of God.

Pinned up on my notice board at home I have this quote from CS Lewis:

"No man who values originality will ever be original. But try to tell the truth as you see it, try to do any bit of work as well as it can be done for the work's sake, and what men call originality will come unsought."

Later he said, in that very Lewis way he has, that we "shouldn't care twopence" if

 what we are saying has been said before. It can still be original, imaginative.

Obviously, he's not talking about the thoughtless repetition of well-turned clichés, or the constant exhumation of dogmas where rigor mortis has long since set in. Or the handing out of propositions which shrinkwrap the mystery of God or the life of faith into convenient parcels. No, it's about talking out, and living out our serial encounters with God in a way that resonate not only with scripture and the narrative of the Church's teaching, but also to our lived experience. We inhale and are enlivened by the truths we find in our unfolding understanding of the universe, and indeed the truths we learn from others who are beyond our faith or tradition. And what we learn from movies, and music and poetry and paintings, and earth and water and air and fire.

That means we have to take risks. In this we are inspired by God, the greatest risk-taker of them all. By making something

where the there was nothing,
God opened herself to pain,
hurt and disappointment. God
opened the door, it seems, right
from the beginning and in the
very process of creation itself, to suffering
and death in order for there to be a world
where there was genuine choice and
authentic freedom. And in the life, death
and resurrection of Jesus we see, even
more clearly the risk of God in demon-
strating his compassion and vulnerability.

It is a risk to give rein to our imaginations.
Because then we start having to think what
it might be like to be someone we despise.
To allow them to be God's children too.

But this process of breathing air in and out
isn't simply a question of us inhaling and
exhaling in our own little air pocket. We
all share the same airspace. That means,
of course, there are breath and wind issues
in confined quarters. Once you share a
bed with someone this becomes only too
real.

Have you ever come across someone whose certainty, or whose ego sucks out all the oxygen from the room and leaves you no room to breathe? These people are so inflated by their own beliefs, or their own selves that they simply corral you into their world and their thinking, leaving no room for denial – and you're left gasping: "but, but, but…"

It strikes me that a really important element of the way we breathe out our lives imaginatively is to understand that we all need air. So much of our idea of health is linked to airiness, to fresh air, the open air, to clearing the air. This means giving one another room to breathe. It's not always easy.

Confession time. I think astrology is rubbish. I just don't get it. OK, I'm prepared to assent to the fact that who we are and how we behave is due to a complex of influences and, that the movement of objects in the universe could be part of that package. But seeing your star sign as a significant determinant of your personality? Can't see it. A friend of mine, huge brain, big fan of Richard Dawkins, starts talking about how much of a Leo he is. I'm about to unload with both barrels, but then I think, take a breath, I'm about to invade his airspace. There may be a time when we can debate this, but now's not the moment.

There are definitely moments when we need to hold fire in a conversation, to let the fresh and holy spirit of agnosticism give breathing space to someone else. Don't get me wrong, I think it's important sometimes for the sparks to fly, to challenge one another, to ask candid questions and to be direct. To wrestle an idea into submission. But there's also a time just to go "mmmm, interesting".

In his poem *I'm the One Who Has the Body* Indian poet, Devara Dasimayya, talks about, "the miracle of [God's] breath in my body". When we breathe, the air travels down our windpipe and into our

 lungs, it ends up in air sacs with thin walls called alveoli, from where the oxygen is absorbed into the blood stream. Air becomes an indivisible part of us.

The inspiring breath of God is absorbed into our very being, making us natural makers, able to hope, alive and alert every minute to the myriad possibilities that surround us. Possibilities triggered by that sacred question: "what would happen if…?"

What would happen if you kissed him?
What would happen if you said goodbye?
What would happen if you made a plan?
What would happen if you turned
left instead of right?
What would happen if you put
that dream into action?
What would happen if you added a
chopped anchovy?

Take a deep breath. Let God inspire you. Use your imagination. Make something of your life.

"God is a consuming fire, and each of us sparks and crackles and fizzes with the same combustible stuff. Everyone is ready to burst into flame."

Fire

In the cool Autumn evening I lay on the ground, in the dark, in the garden. A few feet away, Evan, 14, lay on the grass facing me. I blew into the night air. He blew.

There had been only the faintest hint of combustion in the pile of leaves lying between us but as we huffed and puffed, suddenly the quiet, hidden spark inside the mound burst into life. And then a conflagration: the leaves devoured in bright

 flames of red and blue. Sparks leaping as miniature electrified angels, smoke rising from the floor of the garden like a small volcano.

The more leaves we poured on, the more it blazed, until our ambition got the better of us. We loaded on too many and the fire suffocated in its own fuel. The heat and light was gone, leaving only that lovely burnt autumn smell, and a faint spark of light to remind us what a fire was like. We got back down on the grass again and started blowing.

About 15 billion years ago there was a fire in the middle of nowhere, which was so hot that the universe exploded into being. Roughly speaking, you could call this the scientific explanation for why we are here. Sometimes it's called "the big bang", a soundbite to capture a moment when *nothing* somehow became warm enough to be *something*.

About 15 billions years later –
maybe three thousand years ago
– a shepherd called Moses,
came upon a strange-looking
bush which appeared to be on
fire…..

"I am God", came the voice within the
bushy inferno, "I've seen the people's
troubles, and you Moses are going to
execute my rescue plan."

Moses, not convinced, asked the bush for
some ID. The fire replied with one of the
most famous phrases in religious literature.
The fire says, "I am who I am. If anyone
inquires, tell them, I Am has sent you."
Ask a scientist what blew on the nothing to
create the something that is our universe,
and she will say the question doesn't bear
examination. Before the start, there was
nothing, otherwise, it wouldn't have been
the start. It would have been the second
bit. Or the third bit. Religion is not so
different. If you ask, as children do, "who
made God?" there is no clever answer.
Only this, after a short period of

mumbling: "Er, well…God just is." Which is another way of saying, "I am who I am…"

But where science and faith agree, is that there is a fire at the heart of all existence. In the language of faith, we believe that without this warmth of divine presence each of us will freeze to death. God, as it says elsewhere in the Good Book, is "a consuming fire". And each of us carries within us the divine spark.

This kind of language can disturb some Christians. Perhaps it sounds suspect, because the spark is a common idea in other great faith narratives like Hinduism or Sufism – and Christians like to think that Christianity does not overlap with other religions. Or because it was common in an early opponent of the first Christians, Gnosticism, or in the growing popularity of traditions like the mystical Kabbalah in Judaism.

But replace the word 'spark' with the word 'image', and say we are made in the divine

image and we're all OK again.
God is a consuming fire and
each of us sparks and crackles
and fizzes with the same combustible stuff. Everyone is ready
to burst into flame… but the spark needs
blowing on.

I remember Tom, a friend of mine, in his
early 20s, bumping around Soho in
London, working as a runner for film
companies. He had no idea what his life
was going to be about until he visited
South Africa where almost by accident, the
spark inside became a flame.

Tom's passion was surfing and in Durban –
on the east coast of Africa, with its long
yellow beaches and the crashing waves of
the Indian Ocean – the surf is always up.
But it wasn't the surf that explained why
he never came back to Britain. On the city
streets, he came across children living
rough, never at school, getting drawn into
crime and drugs and violence, being
abused by the police. Listening to their
stories, first he was curious, then he was

angry and then he became determined. The divine spark was caught in a gust of wind. It flared and fired. The stories of these children set Tom alight. Spontaneous human combustion.

"Something told me that it didn't have to be that way, that children didn't have to live like that. I realised I had a passion to change the way things were…" He decided to stay and see what he could do to help. Today, many children have found a new path in life, been reunited with their communities, received vital healthcare, found the path of education and training. Many now work themselves in helping other street children climb from poverty, set alight by the same flames which illuminated Tom.

But how do you find the thing that will fire your life? The calling that will fan the spark inside. Po Bronson, an American writer, interviewed 900 people who had switched from one path in life to another: a stockbroker who became a fish farmer: an estate agent who opened a craft factory in Central America; a lawyer who became a priest; an astronaut who became a fast food chef (actually, I made that last one up). Almost always he found that the call crept up on people, over time, bit by bit, usually hedged around with doubt and fear. "Most of us don't get epiphanies," he writes "We only get a whisper – a faint urge. That's it. That's the call. It's up to you to do the work of discovery, to connect it to an answer."

So what's your passion? What fires you up? What should you do with your one good life? A friend of mine built up a successful production company in London's west end. As the years passed the business grew, took on more staff, diversified… and he could enjoy the fruits of success. His gift with words had taken him into advertising but he'd always been in two minds about it and in time the disenchantment grew.
Was this it ?

 Something inside him suggested it wasn't. Not that what he was doing was wrong, just that it wasn't quite all of who he was, or even most of who he was. And as he listened to his life over the weeks, the months and then years, his life began to speak to him – and he found it calling him to something else.

Eventually he decided to walk away even though he didn't know what he was going to do, or how he would pay the bills. All he knew was that he had to listen to the call of his heart – even if his heart sometimes spoke like a two-year old child, tugging, nagging, never giving up… but not especially articulate. Today he is on a new road and he doesn't know where it will lead. All he knows is that he's happier. That he was right to listen to his life when it began to call.

Of course, a sense of disappointment at our paid work afflicts all of us at different times, and even thinking about options is a luxury when millions of people must toil long hours in field or factory just to put food on the table or a child in school.

But the question of what really fires us up and what we should do with our lives isn't confined to our job – it's about how we find the life we are being calling to. In biblical times this was apparently more straightforward. The Bible is rammed with 'God-Direct', instant divine messaging which leaves people with little uncertainty about what to do next. Samuel, for example, the boy-prophet who heard the voice of God calling him repeatedly in the night. Or Isaiah, who could say, "I saw the Lord seated on a throne, high and exalted, and the train of his robe filled the temple."

Simon and Andrew were minding their fishing business, when Jesus passed by and called them to follow him. The devout Jew Saul, with his specialty in persecuting the early followers of The Way, was blinded by a fire on the Damascus Road. Unsurprisingly, it altered his career path.

 But the chances are that the experience of people like these will not be our experience. The Bible specialises in the dramatic. It doesn't bother us with, say, the argument that went on between Simon and Andrew before they finally decided they would follow Jesus – the compromises struck in the family about who would catch the fish in their absence… and how they would make up for it. The Gospel writers don't trifle us with Rachel and Jake, who looked Jesus in the eye when he called them and said, "Sorry, Jesus. Can't do it. Nothing personal, but the timing's not good…" Or Benjamin and Martha who needed to think it over: "It's a big decision, leaving behind everything…" Only years later, after that bit of the Bible had gone to press, did they find a fire within and decide to heed the call, to discover another way of being who they were meant to be.

People think of 'vocation' as a religious thing – like deciding to become nuns or priests. 'Vocation' comes from the Latin for 'call' and one of the ways we find the divine call is by asking what fires us up, what gets us going, where do our gifts lie and how can we use them? We can't answer this on our own. Sometimes someone else needs to tell us. It was children on the street who unwittingly showed Tom what fired him up.

Although we are often told that 'truth' in the Bible is propositional – things to believe in, concepts to grapple with, doctrines to assent to – another perspective is to say that truth is relational. Not just factual, but personal. As the community theologian Ann Morisy puts it in *Journeying Out*, Jesus didn't say "I speak the truth", he said, "I am the truth…" The earliest followers found their calling in friendship with him, probably more slowly and haltingly than the record suggests. In community with him, they heard the first whisper, sensed the faint urge of another kind of calling.

We discover the truth about ourselves through encountering the other… for example in the friendship networks of a place like a church. In prayer and

 listening, in conversation and collaboration. We run our ideas by our friends and loved ones. We measure their reactions. We wait to see if sparks fly. We begin to find out who we should be, what fires us up. Not just in the working day, but in the rest of the day.

What fires you up ? Think about it, say some prayers about it, talk it through with those you trust. Test your feelings on others, look to the community for inspiration and the call will become clearer. A fourth century north African monk called Augustine put it well, when he said, "You have made us for yourself and our hearts are restless until they find their rest in you." Ask Augustine what he means by that and he has one other piece of advice. He says, "Love … and do what you like."

As Tom puts it, "I realized I had a passion to change things." The sage and gardener Sam Murphy, presently unpublished, spends a lot of time time volunteering in different gardens – kneeling at a flowerbed, pushing a mower, pruning a rose. "I just like it," he says, "I just enjoy it. I like being with the earth and watching God send the sun and the rain and then seeing how everything grows. Sometimes I just like to look at the roses and marvel at them."

Somewhere along the line, Sam found his call. He listened to his life. The spark inside caught fire. He loves God and does what he likes. What fires you up? Lie on the ground, in the dark. And blow on the sparks. Watch the flames leap.

Love God... and do what you like.